Two Sides of a Single Stem

Ja'Shaun Coley

Published by Ja'Shaun Coley, 2026.

TWO SIDES OF A SINGLE STEM

First edition. January 9, 2026.

ISBN: 979-8233158834

Written by Ja'Shaun Coley.

Table of Contents

The Soil of Silence

There is a world that exists beneath the bottom of my shoes. Most people look at a garden and see the colors—the vibrant reds, the reaching yellows, the steady greens. They see the result of growth. But I have spent a lot of time thinking about the dirt. I think about the soil of silence where everything starts.

For me, silence isn't just the absence of noise; it's a heavy, thick layer of everything I don't say. When you struggle with your mental health, especially as a young person, you learn to become an expert in burial. You bury the "bad" days. You bury the "weird" thoughts. You bury the moments where your heart feels like it's beating a rhythm you don't recognize. You pack the dirt down tight so that the surface looks level, so that nobody trips over the uneven ground of your mind.

This soil is where my secrets live. It's where the "Two Sides" began. On the surface, I am standing tall, walking through the halls, and answering questions. But underneath, there is a complex network of roots trying to find enough room to breathe. The silence can be protective—it keeps the world out—but it can also be suffocating. If you keep everything in the dark for too long, the roots begin to tangle.

We are taught that growth is the only thing that matters, but we rarely talk about the environment that growth requires. Sometimes, my soil feels too dry, like I've run out of the energy to keep going. Other times, it feels oversaturated, like I'm drowning in my own emotions. But even in the silence, something is happening. The first step to healing isn't blooming for an audience; it's acknowledging the dirt. It's looking at the parts of ourselves we've buried and realizing that even in the dark, even in the silence, we are still alive. We are still a single stem, even if the world only sees the half that's above the ground.

Midnight Petals

Most flowers wait for the sun to show themselves. They open up when the light hits them, basking in the warmth and the attention of the day. But anxiety doesn't work like that. Anxiety is a midnight petal. It's the flower that blooms when the rest of the world has gone to sleep, opening up in the cold, quiet hours of the night when there's nothing to distract you from the sound of your own thoughts.

When I lay in bed, the "Visible Bloom" that I presented to the world all day starts to fade, and the internal reality takes over. This is when the racing thoughts begin. In the dark, every small worry becomes a giant vine, twisting around my chest. I think about things I said three years ago. I think about things I might have to do three years from now. I wonder if I'm doing enough, if I'm being enough, or if the people I love are seeing the "real" me or just the version I've practiced.

These midnight petals are beautiful in a haunting way, but they are exhausting. While everyone else is recharging, I am working overtime in a garden of "what-ifs." This is the side of the stem that people don't see. They see me the next morning, maybe a little tired, maybe a little quiet, but they don't see the full-bloom panic that happened at 2:00 AM.

I've learned that you can't fight the night by pretending it's day. You have to learn to sit with the midnight petals. You have to realize that the dark doesn't make the thoughts true; it just makes them louder.

My anxiety wants me to believe that the nighttime version of my life is the only reality, but I have to remember that I am the stem that holds both the sunlight and the shadows. I am learning to breathe through the dark, waiting for the petals to close so I can find the rest I deserve.

The Weighted Root

Depression is often described as a cloud or a fog, but for me, it has always felt more like a weighted root. It's the sensation of being anchored to the ground so heavily that even the idea of reaching for the light feels impossible.

In a garden, roots are supposed to be the source of strength. They hold the plant steady. But when you're dealing with depression, your foundation feels like lead. It's a gravity that exists only for you. You watch other people move through their days with a lightness that feels foreign. They "sprout" with ease—they get out of bed, they laugh at jokes, they make plans. Meanwhile, my roots feel like they are pulling me deeper into the earth, demanding all my energy just to stay upright.

This is the hidden side of the stem. On the outside, people might just think I'm "lazy" or "tired." They see a flower that isn't opening and assume it just needs more water or more sun. They don't realize that the struggle isn't with the atmosphere; it's with the anchor. The weight is internal. It's a heaviness in the limbs and a silence in the soul.

The hardest part of the weighted root is the guilt. I feel like I *should* be blooming. I see the "Single Stem" and I hate the part of me that is stuck in the mud. But I'm trying to be kinder to my roots. I'm learning that even a weighted root is a living thing. Sometimes, staying grounded is the most productive thing you can do. You don't always have to be reaching for the sky to be valuable. Sometimes, just surviving the weight is its own kind of growth. I am more than just my ability to bloom; I am the strength it takes to hold on when the ground feels like it's trying to swallow me whole.

Ancestral Dirt

We like to think that we start as a clean slate, a fresh seed planted in a brand new pot. But the truth is, we are often planted in "ancestral dirt." We inherit the soil that our parents, and their parents, lived in. Sometimes that soil is rich with resilience and love, but other times, it comes with rocks and acidity that we didn't ask for.

When I look at my own mental health, I have to look at the dirt I was given. I see patterns of worry that didn't start with me. I see silences that have been passed down like heirlooms. It's a strange feeling to realize that some of the "weeds" in my mind were actually planted generations ago. Maybe someone else had PTSD and didn't have the words for it. Maybe someone else lived with a weighted root for forty years and just called it "being tired."

This doesn't mean we are stuck. It just means we have to understand the chemistry of our soil. If your dirt is acidic, you have to find ways to balance it. You have to learn which parts of your history are worth keeping and which parts are just rocks that are making it hard for your roots to grow. I am learning to sift through the ancestral dirt. I'm keeping the strength and the stories, but I'm working hard to clear out the stones of old trauma. I am the gardener of my own life now, and even if I didn't choose where I was planted, I get to choose how I treat the ground I'm standing on.

Dormant Seeds

There are seasons in my life where it feels like absolutely nothing is happening. I look at other people and they are blooming, growing new leaves, and reaching for the sky. Meanwhile, I feel like a dormant seed. I am stuck under the surface, invisible and still.

In a world that values "productivity" and "constant growth," being dormant feels like failing. We are told that if we aren't moving forward, we are falling behind. But nature tells a different story. Every flower needs a period of dormancy. Every seed needs a time of quiet before it can sprout. For me, these are the days when my depression or my exhaustion takes over. I can't "perform" for the world. I can't smile or pretend. I just have to sit in the dark and wait.

I'm trying to stop seeing these quiet times as wasted time. Just because you can't see the growth doesn't mean it isn't happening. Deep inside the seed, the chemistry is changing. The energy is being gathered. Dormancy is a form of survival. It's the way we protect ourselves when the environment is too harsh. If you try to force a bloom in the middle of a freeze, the plant will die. So, I am learning to trust the stillness. I am learning that "being" is just as important as "doing." I am a dormant seed, and when the timing is right, the growth will come. Until then, the dark is just a place to rest.

The Taproot of Memory

If you pull up a weed, you'll see one long, thick root that goes deeper than all the others. That's the taproot. In my mind, the taproot is memory. It's the one event, the one feeling, or the one period of my life that everything else is anchored to.

When you live with PTSD, your taproot is often a memory that you wish you could just cut off. It's the "foundational" moment that created the anxiety or the fear. No matter how much I grow or how many new "leaves" I sprout, that taproot is still there, pulling nutrients from a past I'd rather forget. It's frustrating because it feels like I'm always tied to something that happened a long time ago.

But I'm learning that you don't have to let the taproot poison the rest of the plant. You can't always remove the memory—it's part of your structure now—but you can change how much power you give it. I am learning to grow secondary roots. I am building new foundations based on who I am today, not just who I was then. The taproot of memory might be deep, but it doesn't have to be the only thing holding me up. I am more than just my past; I am the entire system of roots that I am building every single day.

Underground Echoes

The hardest part about the "Internal Root" side of the stem is the noise. Most people think roots are silent, but in my head, the underground is a place of echoes. These are the things I say to myself when no one is listening. *You aren't doing enough. Everyone is judging you. You're going to fail.*

These underground echoes are like a feedback loop. They start small, but they bounce off the walls of my mind until they are deafening. This is where my anxiety lives. It creates a narrative that I'm forced to listen to all day. While I'm sitting in class or talking to friends, the echoes are humming underneath. It makes it hard to focus, and it makes it even harder to believe the good things people say to me.

I've started to realize that the echoes aren't the truth—they are just sound. They are reflections of my fears, not reflections of my reality. I'm learning to talk back to the echoes. When the voice says, "You're a failure," I try to remind myself of a small win. When it says, "Nobody likes you," I think of one person who does. It's a slow process, like trying to dampen the sound in a cavern, but it's working. The more I fill my "underground" with kindness, the softer the echoes become.

Nutrients of Hope

To grow, a plant needs more than just dirt; it needs nutrients. Nitrogen, phosphorus, potassium—the invisible things that make the difference between a wilting stem and a strong one. For me, hope is the nutrient. But when you're struggling with your mental health, hope isn't a big, glowing light. It's something much smaller.

Hope is a nutrient I have to find in tiny doses. It's the way the sun feels on my skin for five minutes. It's a text from a friend that doesn't require an answer. It's the feeling of finishing a book or finally making my bed. These things might seem insignificant to others, but for me, they are the chemicals that keep my roots alive. They are the small bits of "good" that I can absorb when the rest of the world feels "bad."

I used to wait for a "miracle" to feel better, but now I'm looking for nutrients. I'm looking for the small, daily things that help me survive. You can't bloom on an empty stomach, and you can't heal on an empty soul. I am learning to be intentional about what I let into my root system. I am feeding myself hope, one tiny bit at a time, until the stem is strong enough to reach for the light.

The Dark Basement

Depression can feel like being trapped in a dark basement. You know there is a house above you. You can hear people walking around, laughing, and living their lives in the light. But you are down here, and you can't find the stairs. The air is heavy, and the shadows feel like they are part of your own skin.

This is the most isolated side of the single stem. In the "Dark Basement," I feel completely cut off from the person I am "supposed" to be. I feel like a ghost in my own life. The hardest part isn't the darkness itself; it's the knowledge that the light exists and I just can't get to it. It's a feeling of profound loneliness, even when people are right there in the room with me.

But even in a basement, there is a foundation. I've realized that the basement is part of the house, too. It's not a separate place; it's just the lowest level. And just because I'm in the basement today doesn't mean I've moved out of the house. I am learning to wait out the darkness. I am learning that I don't always have to find the stairs by myself. Sometimes, just staying in the basement and breathing is enough. Eventually, someone opens a door, or a little light leaks through a crack in the floorboards. I am staying in the house, even when I'm on the bottom floor.

Tangled Threads

Sometimes my emotions don't feel like separate things. They aren't just "sad" or "angry" or "scared." Instead, they are a mess of tangled threads. I feel anxious because I'm depressed, and I'm depressed because I'm anxious, and then I'm frustrated because I'm both. It's like a ball of yarn that a cat has played with—everything is knotted together so tightly that you can't find the beginning or the end.

This tangling happens "underground." On the surface, I might just look "moody." But inside, I'm trying to untie knots that feel impossible. I try to pull on one thread to understand it, and it just makes three other knots tighter. It's exhausting to live with a mind that feels like a puzzle you can't solve.

I'm learning that I don't have to untangle everything at once. Sometimes, you just have to look at one small knot and breathe through it. You have to accept that emotions are messy and that it's okay to feel three things at the same time. I am a single stem, but that stem is made of many different fibers. The tangles are part of my complexity. I don't need to be perfectly "straight" or "organized" to be beautiful. I am learning to love the mess, even while I'm working to simplify it.

Oxygen Deprivation

Anxiety feels like oxygen deprivation. It's the feeling of your lungs working perfectly fine, but the air just isn't "getting in." It's a physical panic that starts in the chest and moves into the throat, a tightening that makes the world feel very small and very dangerous.

When I'm in this state, my internal roots are screaming. It's like a plant that has been overwatered and the roots are starting to rot because they can't get any air. My brain goes into "survival mode." I can't think about the future or the past; I can only think about the next breath. This is the side of the stem that feels the most fragile. It feels like at any moment, the stem could just snap under the pressure.

The only way I've found to fight the oxygen deprivation is to slow down. I have to force my roots to wait. I focus on the ground under my feet—literally. I feel the weight of my body. I count to four. I remind myself that I am safe, even if I don't *feel* safe. Anxiety tries to steal my breath, but I am learning how to take it back. I am finding the "pockets of air" in my day, the moments where I can just *be* without the pressure. I am breathing, even when it's hard.

The First Sprout

Healing doesn't happen all at once. It's not like you wake up one day and the depression is gone and the anxiety is solved. Instead, it happens in "first sprouts." It's that tiny, microscopic bit of green that breaks through the soil after a long winter. It's fragile, and it's easily crushed, but it's the most important thing in the world.

The first sprout is the moment I decide to try again. It's the first time I laugh and actually mean it. It's the first morning I wake up and the "Weighted Root" feels a little bit lighter. These moments are scary because they feel like they won't last. I'm always afraid that a "Sudden Frost" will come and kill the new growth. But the sprout is proof of life. It's proof that all that time I spent "dormant" or "weighted" wasn't for nothing.

This essay marks the end of the "Internal World" section because the sprout is where the two sides meet. It's the point where the root finally touches the light. I am still the same stem, and I still have all that history underground, but I am finally breaking the surface. I am starting to see the world, and more importantly, I am letting the world see me. It's just a tiny sprout for now, but it's a beginning. And every beautiful flower started as nothing more than a brave bit of green pushing through the dirt.

Sharp Edges

When you look at a rose, the first thing you notice is the bloom. But the second thing you notice—the thing that keeps you from grabbing it too tightly—is the thorns. For a long time, I hated the thorns in my own personality. I hated the way I could be sharp, the way I could snap at someone I love, or the way I could use my words like a blade to push people away.

But I've started to realize that thorns aren't there because the flower is "mean." Thorns are there because the flower is valuable and vulnerable. When you've been hurt, or when you live with the constant hyper-vigilance of PTSD, your brain develops sharp edges to keep the world at a distance. Anger isn't always just anger; sometimes it's a shield. It's a way of saying, *don't come any closer, because I don't know if I can handle being touched right now.*

The problem is that thorns don't choose who they prick. Sometimes I hurt the people who are just trying to water me. I see the look in their eyes when I get defensive, and it adds a layer of guilt to my soil. But I am learning to explain my edges. I am learning to say, "I'm feeling sharp today," so they know it's not about them. My thorns are part of my survival, but I'm working on making sure they don't keep out the very things I need to grow.

A Storm in the Garden

A PTSD trigger is like a sudden, violent storm in a garden that was perfectly calm just a second ago. One moment the sun is out and the leaves are still, and the next, the wind is tearing at the petals and the rain is flooding the roots. The worst part is that the storm doesn't come from the sky; it comes from inside the stem.

When I am triggered, my body forgets that I am safe in the present. It thinks I am back in the past, back in the moment where the trauma first took root. The "Two Sides" of my existence collide in a way that feels like a physical crash. My heart starts to race, my breath gets short, and I feel a desperate need to run or hide. To an outsider, it might look like I'm overreacting to something small—a sound, a smell, a specific word—but they don't see the hurricane happening behind my eyes.

Surviving the storm takes everything I have. I have to hold onto the "Stem" with both hands and wait for the wind to die down. I try to ground myself by naming things I can see or touch, trying to remind my brain that the storm isn't real, even though it feels like it's breaking me. When it finally passes, I am usually exhausted and wilted. But I am still standing. The petals might be a little bruised, but the roots held. I am learning that the storm doesn't define the garden; the recovery does.

The Bristle Effect

Have you ever seen a plant that curls up or bristles when you touch it? It's an immediate, reflexive reaction. In my life, I call this the "Bristle Effect." It's the way my anxiety makes me react to things before my conscious mind even has a chance to process what's happening.

If someone stands too close to me in line, I bristle. If a teacher calls on me unexpectedly, I bristle. If a door slams down the hall, I bristle. It's an automatic tightening of the muscles, a sudden spike in adrenaline that prepares me for a fight that isn't coming. It's exhausting to live in a body that is always "on guard," always expecting a threat.

I used to be embarrassed by how jumpy I was. I felt like I was "broken" because I couldn't just relax. But now I see the bristle as a form of communication. My body is trying to tell me that it feels unsafe. Instead of getting mad at myself for bristling, I'm trying to listen. I'm trying to create an environment where my body doesn't feel like it has to be a cactus all the time. I'm slowly teaching my "Stem" that it's okay to let its guard down, one deep breath at a time.

Barriers of Stem

Sometimes, the best way to stay safe is to just stop growing toward anyone else. I call this "Barriers of Stem." It's the period where I pull all my energy inward and refuse to let anyone in. I stop answering texts, I give one-word answers, and I stay in my room where the walls are predictable.

Isolation is a complicated thorn. It feels safe because no one can hurt you if they can't get to you. But it also keeps out the light. When I build these barriers, I am essentially putting myself in a dark box. I am protecting the bloom, but I am starving the roots. Depression loves these barriers; it thrives in the quiet, lonely spaces where it can tell me that I'm better off alone.

Breaking through my own barriers is one of the hardest things I do. It feels like trying to push through a thicket of my own making. But I've realized that a single stem can't survive in a vacuum. We need the "cross-pollination" of friendship and connection to stay healthy. I'm trying to build "gates" instead of walls—ways to let people in when I'm ready, without feeling like I've lost my protection entirely.

Venom in the Sap

Every plant has sap—the lifeblood that carries nutrients from the roots to the leaves. But sometimes, the sap can become toxic. In my mental health journey, the "Venom in the Sap" is toxic self-talk. It's the way I talk to myself when I'm struggling, the "internal poison" that tells me I'm not worth the effort it takes to heal.

This venom is quiet. It doesn't scream; it just flows through every thought. *You're a burden. You're never going to get better. Everyone would be happier if you weren't so difficult.* When these thoughts become part of my "circulation," everything starts to wilt. I could have the best day ever, but if the venom is flowing, I won't be able to feel the joy of it.

Fighting this internal poison requires a total "flush" of the system. I have to replace the venom with truth. I have to remind myself that my illness is not my identity. I have to practice self-compassion, even when it feels "fake." It's like cleaning out a clogged pipe; it takes time and patience. But the more I feed myself kindness, the thinner the venom becomes, until the sap is clear again and I can finally feel the nutrients of life.

The Prickly Pear

There are days when I am simply difficult to love. I am irritable, I am quiet, and I am prickly. On these days, I feel like a prickly pear cactus—covered in tiny, invisible needles that hurt anyone who tries to get close. I want the hug, but I push the person away. I want the conversation, but I start an argument instead.

This is the most painful part of the "Thorns" section. It's the way my mental health affects the people I care about. I see their frustration, and I see their hurt, and it makes me want to grow even more needles to protect them from *me*. It's a vicious cycle: I feel bad, so I act out, then I feel worse because I acted out, so I act out again.

The only way out of the "Prickly Pear" phase is honesty. I have to be brave enough to say, "I am hurting right now, and it's making me act like I don't want you here, but I do." I have to ask for patience when I don't deserve it. And I have to remember that the people who love me see the fruit, not just the needles. They know that underneath the prickliness, there is still a sweet, valuable soul worth holding onto.

Armor of Petals

There is a specific kind of strength in looking soft while feeling like steel. I call this "Armor of Petals." It's the version of me that goes to school, does the work, and smiles at the right times, all while my internal world is a battlefield. People see the "petals"—the kindness, the humor, the cooperation—and they think I am doing great. They don't realize those petals are actually scales of armor.

This is a defense mechanism born out of the need to survive in a world that doesn't always have room for "broken" things. If I look okay, people won't ask questions I can't answer. If I look okay, I won't have to explain why I cried in the bathroom for ten minutes. But wearing armor is heavy. By the time I get home, my shoulders ache from the weight of the performance.

The "Two Sides" are at their most extreme here. The "Visible Bloom" is a masterpiece of deception, and the "Internal Root" is screaming for a break. I'm learning that I don't always have to wear the armor. I'm finding "safe gardens"—people and places where I can drop the petals and just be the bruised, tired stem that I am. True strength isn't just about how much armor you can wear; it's about having the courage to take it off.

Sudden Frost

Sometimes, my mental health shifts without warning. I can be having a perfectly fine morning—sunshine on the leaves, birds singing—and then, for no apparent reason, the "Sudden Frost" hits. A wave of sadness or a spike of panic washes over me, and everything turns cold. The colors of the day seem to grey out, and I feel a shiver in my soul that I can't shake.

This is one of the scariest parts of living with depression and anxiety. The lack of "reason" makes me feel out of control. If I knew *why* I felt bad, I could fix it. But when the frost comes out of nowhere, I feel helpless. I worry that I'll never be warm again, that this coldness is my new permanent state.

I'm learning to treat the "Sudden Frost" like a weather pattern. You can't stop the frost, but you can prepare for it. I keep "emergency blankets" in my mind—comforting movies, favorite songs, a list of things I know are true even when I can't feel them. I remind myself that frost is temporary. The sun will come back up eventually. I just have to hunker down, keep my roots warm, and wait for the thaw.

The Thistle's Vow

A thistle is a plant that has decided it will never be eaten, never be crushed, and never be ignored. It is a vow of defiance. In my journey, "The Thistle's Vow" is the promise I made to myself after I was hurt: *I will never let anyone get that close again. I will never be that vulnerable again.*

It's a vow of safety, but it's also a vow of loneliness. When you decide to be a thistle, you are choosing protection over connection. You are choosing the "Thorns" as your primary identity. For a while, this felt like power. I felt untouchable. But after a while, I realized that I was also untouching. I was safe, but I was static. I wasn't growing; I was just defending.

I'm working on softening the vow. I'm trying to realize that being hurt is a risk of being alive, and that the "Single Stem" is meant to do more than just survive—it's meant to experience the world. I'm trading the thistle's vow for a "vow of boundaries." I will protect myself, yes, but I will also leave enough space for someone to reach out and touch a leaf without getting pricked.

Invasive Vines

Intrusive thoughts are like invasive vines—kudzu or ivy that starts as a tiny sprout and suddenly takes over the entire garden. They wrap around the "Stem" and start to choke it. They whisper things like, *What if you did something terrible? What if something horrible happens to your family?* These thoughts aren't "me," but they are in my head, and they feel incredibly real.

The "Thorns" in this essay are the sharp, clinging parts of these thoughts. They are hard to pull off once they've latched on. They make me feel guilty for things I haven't even done. They make me feel "crazy" or "evil." But I'm learning about the biology of the mind. Intrusive thoughts are just "brain glitches"—junk mail that my mind is sending me.

I'm learning not to water the invasive vines. When a thought pops up, instead of fighting it (which just gives it more energy), I try to just acknowledge it. "Oh, there's that vine again." I don't let it wrap around my stem. I focus on the "Internal Root" and the "Visible Bloom" that I know are real. The vines might still be there, but they aren't the boss of the garden. I am.

The Scrape of Reality

Coming down from a high-anxiety moment or a panic attack feels like a "Scrape." It's the physical and emotional soreness that follows a period of intense "Thorns." Your body has been in "fight or flight" mode for so long that when you finally land back in reality, you feel raw and exposed.

Everything feels a little too loud, a little too bright. You feel embarrassed about the "scene" you might have made, even if no one saw it. You feel like a plant that has been dragged across the pavement—your leaves are torn and your stem is bent. This is a very vulnerable "side" of the stem. You aren't in the "Hidden Roots" anymore, and you aren't in the "Visible Bloom." You are just... hurt.

This is the time for "Gently Replanting." I have to be very careful with myself during the scrape. I need quiet, I need soft things, and I need to not judge myself for how I feel. I'm learning that the "Scrape" is a sign that the danger is over. The pain is part of the healing. I am finding my way back to the dirt, back to the safety of the garden, where I can slowly start to repair the damage.

Defensive Growth

Sometimes, a plant will grow in a strange, twisted way because it's trying to avoid an obstacle. If there's a rock in the way, the root goes around it. If there's a wall, the stem leans away. This is "Defensive Growth." In my life, this is the way my personality has been shaped by my struggles.

I am the person I am because I had to learn how to survive. My humor is a way to deflect tension. My empathy comes from knowing what it feels like to be in the "Dark Basement." My "Thorns" are just the way I've adapted to the environment I was given. It's not "pretty" growth, and it's not "perfect" growth, but it is *my* growth.

I'm starting to appreciate the "twists" in my stem. They make me unique. They are the map of my survival. I don't want to be a "straight" flower anymore—that person wouldn't have the perspective I have. I am proud of the defensive growth. It shows that no matter what "rocks" were put in my way, I found a way to keep reaching for the sun.

The Breaking Branch

This is the hardest essay in the "Thorns" section because it's about the moment where the pressure becomes too much. Every stem has a breaking point. Every branch can only hold so much weight before it snaps. There are days when the "Weighted Root," the "Sudden Frost," and the "Invasive Vines" all happen at once, and I simply break.

Breaking isn't a failure. It's a biological reality. It's what happens when the environment is harsher than the plant's capacity to handle it. When I break, I can't "bloom" or "thrive." I can only fall. For a long time, I was terrified of breaking. I thought it meant I was "weak." But I've learned that a broken branch isn't the end of the tree.

In nature, a break is often a place where new growth starts. It's a "pruning" that happened without my consent, but it clears the way for something stronger to emerge. When I break, I have to go back to the "Hidden Roots." I have to rest. I have to let the "Single Stem" heal. This is the halfway point of our journey—the moment where we realize that we can't survive on "Thorns" alone. We have to find a new way to live. We have to move toward the "Visible Bloom," not as a mask, but as a true expression of our survival.

The Paper Flower

There is a specific kind of beauty in a paper flower. It never wilts, it never needs water, and its colors stay vibrant no matter how dark the room gets. From a distance, it looks perfect—maybe even better than a real flower. But if you get close enough to touch it, you realize the truth: it's hollow. It has no scent, no life, and no roots. It is an imitation of growth.

In my life, I have spent many days being a paper flower. I show up to school with my hair done, my clothes neat, and my "I'm fine" script ready to go. I look like the picture of health. I look like someone who has their life together. But inside, I feel artificial. I am performing a version of "Ja'Shaun" that is easy for people to handle. A paper flower doesn't have "Weighted Roots" or "Sudden Frost." It just exists to be looked at.

The danger of being a paper flower is that people stop checking on you. They see the vibrant colors and assume the garden is thriving. They don't realize that under the bright exterior, I am starving for something real. I am tired of being a prop in my own life. I want to be a living thing, even if that means I have to show my bruises and my wilting leaves. I would rather be a real weed than a perfect paper rose.

Artificial Sunlight

We live in a world of artificial sunlight. We carry it in our pockets, a glow that emanates from our screens, telling us how we should look, what we should be doing, and how "happy" everyone else is. For me, social media is the brightest source of this light, and it's also the most blinding.

When I post a photo, I am selecting a tiny, curated "petal" of my life and presenting it as the whole bloom. I use filters to smooth out the "Thorns" and captions to hide the "Hidden Roots." The "Artificial Sunlight" of likes and comments feels good for a second, but it doesn't actually help me grow. It's like a plant trying to photosynthesize under a desk lamp; it might keep you alive for a while, but it won't make you strong.

I find myself comparing my "Internal Root" to everyone else's "Visible Bloom." I see their highlight reels and feel like a failure because my garden is messy. I have to remind myself that everyone is using a filter. Everyone is standing in the artificial light. I am learning to put the phone down and find the real sun—the kind that warms the skin and reaches all the way down to the dirt.

The Public Garden

Being in public when you struggle with anxiety or depression feels like being a specimen in a botanical garden. There are signs everywhere telling people how to look at you, but no one is allowed to touch. You are on display, expected to be "beautiful" and "functional" for the enjoyment of the crowd.

In the "Public Garden" of high school or social events, I feel the weight of every pair of eyes. I worry that people can see the "Tangled Threads" of my mind just by looking at my face. I feel like I have to stand perfectly still, keeping my "Stem" straight so no one notices the lean. It is a performance that requires constant maintenance, a high-stakes game of "pretend" that leaves me gasping for air by the end of the day.

The pressure to perform for society is one of the heaviest "Thorns" I carry. I wish I could just be a wildflower in the woods, growing for myself without the need for an audience. I am learning that I don't owe the world a perfect bloom. My value isn't measured by how many people admire my petals. I am allowed to be a private garden, with gates that I only open for the people I trust.

Manicured Lawns

There is something unsettling about a perfectly manicured lawn. Every blade of grass is the same height, every edge is trimmed, and not a single dandelion is allowed to exist. It looks orderly, but it's unnatural. It takes a massive amount of chemicals and labor to keep it that way.

I used to try to be a manicured lawn. I was obsessed with perfectionism because I thought if I looked "tidy," no one would look deeper and find the mess. I trimmed away my personality, suppressed my "weird" thoughts, and poisoned my own "weeds" of sadness before they could sprout. I wanted to be a surface that was easy to walk on, someone who never caused a problem or needed extra care.

But perfectionism is a form of self-erasure. By trying to be a "Manicured Lawn," I was killing the very things that made me a living, breathing human. I am learning to love the dandelions. I am letting the edges get a little rough. A garden that is too tidy has no room for life. I am choosing to be a bit "overgrown" if it means I get to keep my soul.

Greenhouse Glass

Greenhouse glass is a strange barrier. It lets the light in, and it keeps the temperature steady, but it's still a wall. You can see the outside world, and the outside world can see you, but there is no actual contact. You are protected, but you are also trapped.

I often feel like I am living behind "Greenhouse Glass." I am "visible"—I am present in conversations, I am doing my work—but I feel untouchable. There is a layer of glass between me and the people I love. I can see them laughing, I can hear them talking, but the sound is muffled. I am in a controlled environment, keeping myself safe from the "Sudden Frost" of the world, but I am also incredibly lonely.

The glass is a defense mechanism. I built it so that nothing could surprise me, nothing could hurt me. But it also keeps out the breeze. It keeps out the rain. I am learning that to truly grow, you have to be willing to step outside the greenhouse. You have to risk the wind. I am slowly tapping on the glass, looking for a way to break through and finally feel the world against my skin.

The Flower Show

Have you ever been to a flower show? It's a whirlwind of colors, scents, and people. It's a celebration of the "Visible Bloom," and it is absolutely exhausting. For me, a "Flower Show" is any day where I have to be "on" for a long time—a family reunion, a school presentation, a birthday party.

I put on my best petals. I project energy I don't actually have. I smile until my face aches and I laugh at things that aren't funny. I am the prize-winning bloom, the center of attention. But the second I get into the car to go home, I crash. The "Flower Show" is a massive drain on my internal root system. I have spent all my "Nutrients of Hope" on a four-hour event, and now I have nothing left for myself.

I'm learning to manage my "Show Schedule." I'm realizing that I can't do a flower show every day. I need "Dirt Days"—days where I don't have to be pretty, days where I can just be a root in the dark. I am learning that it's okay to turn down an invitation if it means saving my energy for my own survival. The bloom is for the world, but the stem is for me.

Floral Arrangement

In a floral arrangement, the flowers are cut and placed into a vase. They are organized to look a certain way, usually to fit a theme or a specific "vibe." They look beautiful, but they are dying. Because they have been cut from their roots, their time is limited.

For a long time, I let other people "arrange" me. My parents, my teachers, my friends—they all had a "vase" they wanted me to fit into. They wanted me to be the "smart one," the "funny one," or the "strong one." I cut off the parts of myself that didn't fit their arrangement. I let them decide which direction I should lean and which other "flowers" I should be grouped with.

But a "Floral Arrangement" is a temporary thing. I don't want to be a cut flower in someone else's vase. I want to be a living plant in my own soil. I am reclaiming my roots. I am growing in directions that might not look "balanced" to others, but they feel right to me. I am not a decoration; I am a single stem, and I decide where I bloom.

Wilted in Plain Sight

There is a tragic kind of invisibility that happens when you are "Wilted in Plain Sight." It's the moments when your leaves are drooping, your colors are fading, and you are clearly struggling, but the people around you just look away. Maybe they are uncomfortable. Maybe they don't know what to say. Or maybe they are so used to your "Visible Bloom" that they refuse to see the decay.

When I am "Wilted in Plain Sight," I feel like I am screaming in a soundproof room. I drop hints—I say I'm "tired," I stop eating, I pull away—but no one acts. They see the struggle, but they treat it like a background detail. It makes me feel like my pain is an inconvenience to their garden. It makes me want to pull my roots up and move to a different world.

I'm learning that I can't wait for people to notice the wilt. I have to be the one to say, "I am dying over here." It's hard to ask for water when you feel like you don't deserve it, but it's the only way to survive. I am learning to find "Gardeners"—people who aren't afraid of the wilt, people who see the fade and reach for the watering can instead of walking away.

The Perfume of Positivity

We are often told to "just stay positive." People offer us "The Perfume of Positivity"—clichés and quotes that are supposed to mask the smell of our struggle. *Everything happens for a reason. What doesn't kill you makes you stronger. Just smile!* It smells sweet for a second, but it doesn't change the fact that something is rotting underneath.

"Toxic Positivity" is a thorn disguised as a petal. It tells us that our "Hidden Roots" are wrong, that we shouldn't feel the way we do. It makes us feel guilty for being depressed or anxious. When I spray myself with this perfume, I am lying to myself. I am pretending that the "Dark Basement" doesn't exist.

I'm throwing away the perfume. I'm learning that it's okay to smell like dirt sometimes. It's okay to be honest about the fact that life is hard and that "positive vibes" aren't enough to fix a chemical imbalance or a deep trauma. I don't need to be "sweet" to be valid. I would rather be honest and stinky than perfect and fake.

Pollinated Gossip

In a garden, bees carry pollen from one flower to another. In a community, gossip works the same way. Stories, rumors, and opinions are carried from person to person, "pollinating" everyone's perception of who you are. When you struggle with your mental health, "Pollinated Gossip" can be devastating.

I've heard the whispers. *Did you hear about what happened to him? I heard he's "crazy." I heard he can't handle the pressure.* These rumors aren't just words; they are "Invasive Vines" that try to rewrite my story. They take the "Two Sides" of my life and turn them into a caricature. People start looking at my "Visible Bloom" and only seeing the things they've heard.

I'm learning that I can't control the bees. People are going to talk, and they are going to get the story wrong. But I can control my own "Nectar." I can stay true to my roots and my truth. Eventually, the gossip dies out, but the stem remains. I am the only one who truly knows what happens "underground," and that is the only opinion that matters.

Watering the Performance

Keeping up a "Visible Bloom" is a full-time job. I call it "Watering the Performance." It's the constant effort of making sure the mask doesn't slip. It's checking my reflection to make sure I look "normal." It's rehearsing conversations so I don't sound "depressed." It's an investment of energy that I really should be using for my actual healing.

The irony is that I am watering the very thing that is keeping me from getting better. The more I water the performance, the more people believe I am okay, and the less likely I am to get the help I need. It's a self-sustaining cycle of exhaustion. I am keeping the lie alive while the truth is starving.

I am trying to "under-water" the performance. I am letting the mask slip on purpose. I am being "too quiet" at dinner. I am letting people see that I haven't done my hair. It's terrifying, but it's also a relief. Every time I stop watering the performance, I have more energy for my "Hidden Roots." I am choosing reality over the show.

Sun-Scorched Shoulders

Burnout is the "Sun-Scorched Shoulders" of the mental health journey. It's what happens when you've been standing in the "Public Garden," wearing the "Armor of Petals," and "Watering the Performance" for too long. You've been "the strong one" for so everyone else that you've forgotten how to take care of yourself. You are burnt, dry, and ready to snap.

This is the end of the "Visible Bloom" section because it's the point where the performance fails. You can't be "on" forever. The sun is too hot, and the expectations are too high. When my shoulders are scorched, I can't even pretend to be okay. I just want to go back to the "Soil of Silence" and stay there.

But burnout is also a teacher. It's my body's way of saying, *enough*. It's a forced "Dormancy" that clears the way for a new kind of growth. I am learning to find the "Shade." I am setting boundaries and saying "no." I am realizing that I am not a sun-god; I am just a single stem. And even the strongest stem needs a break from the light.

Photosynthesis

Growth isn't just about avoiding the "Sudden Frost" or fighting off "Invasive Vines." Eventually, you have to find a way to take in the light. In nature, photosynthesis is the process of turning sunlight into energy—literally creating food out of thin air and warmth. For me, healing began when I learned how to do the same with my emotions.

I spent so many years focusing on the "Weighted Root" that I forgot how to absorb the good stuff. I would brush off compliments, ignore small victories, and assume that any moment of happiness was just a fluke. I was starving myself of the very things I needed to get stronger. Photosynthesis is a choice; the plant has to turn its leaves toward the sun. I had to start intentionally looking for things that fed my soul.

I started small. I noticed the way a song made me feel. I noticed the taste of my favorite food. I let myself feel proud when I finished a hard assignment. These tiny bits of "light" are being converted into emotional energy. I am learning that I don't have to wait for a "miracle" to feel better; I just have to keep turning toward the light, one tiny leaf at a time.

Pruning

A garden that is never pruned eventually becomes a tangled mess where nothing can thrive. To grow truly healthy, you have to be willing to cut things away. In therapy, I learned the art of "Pruning." It's the difficult, sometimes painful process of identifying the thoughts, habits, and even relationships that are draining my energy without giving anything back.

Pruning feels like a loss at first. When you cut a branch, the plant looks smaller. It looks like you're going backward. I had to cut away the "Thorns" of toxic self-talk. I had to prune the habit of staying up until 3:00 AM in a "Midnight Petal" panic. I even had to prune some friendships that only bloomed when I was performing for them.

But the result of pruning isn't weakness; it's focus. By cutting away the dead weight, I am giving my "Single Stem" more energy to grow in the right directions. I am no longer wasting my "Nutrients of Hope" on things that don't serve my healing. It hurts to let go, but the new growth that comes afterward is always stronger and more beautiful than what was there before.

The Perennial Soul

There are two kinds of flowers: annuals, which live for one season and then die, and perennials, which return year after year. For a long time, I felt like an annual. I thought that if I had one "Bad Winter"—one major depressive episode or one trauma—it was over for me. I thought the "Single Stem" was too fragile to survive a freeze.

But I am realizing that I am a perennial soul. My roots are deeper than the season. Even when the "Visible Bloom" is gone and I am "Dormant" under the snow, the life inside me is still there. I have survived every winter I've ever faced. I have been "broken," "scorched," and "wilted," and every single time, I have come back when the ground warmed up.

Understanding my perennial nature takes the fear out of the hard days. When the "Sudden Frost" hits now, I don't panic. I know that my roots are strong enough to hold on. I know that this season of darkness is not the end of my story; it's just the part where I gather my strength. I am built for the long haul. I will return, and I will bloom again

New Growth

Healing doesn't look like a finished garden; it looks like "New Growth." It's the tiny, bright green leaves that appear on a branch you thought was dead. For me, new growth shows up in the most unexpected ways. It's the first time I realize I haven't had a panic attack in a week. It's the first time I laugh at a joke and don't feel like I'm "Watering a Performance."

New growth is fragile. It's soft and easily bruised. When I first start feeling better, I'm almost afraid to admit it. I'm waiting for the other shoe to drop, waiting for the "Weighted Root" to pull me back down. But I'm learning to celebrate the sprouts. I'm learning to protect them without smothering them.

Every new leaf is a victory. It's proof that the "Internal Root" and the "Visible Bloom" are finally working together. I am not "fixed," but I am growing. And in a garden, growth is the only thing that matters. I am keeping a tally of the new growth, reminding myself that even on the slow days, I am becoming someone new.

Wildflower Wisdom

Most flowers in a garden are there because someone planted them, watered them, and protected them. But wildflowers are different. They grow in the cracks of the sidewalk, on the sides of highways, and in the middle of abandoned lots. They grow where they aren't "supposed" to be. This is "Wildflower Wisdom."

I've realized that my mental health journey hasn't been a "Manicured Lawn." I've had to grow in some pretty harsh environments. I've had to find "Nutrients of Hope" in places where there wasn't much to go around. For a long time, I felt "less than" because my life didn't look like a prize-winning display. But wildflowers are the toughest plants in the world.

I am a wildflower. I have learned to bloom in the middle of a storm. I have learned to find beauty in the cracks of my own history. My resilience doesn't come from being "perfect"; it comes from my ability to adapt to the dirt I was given. I am proud of my wildness. I am proud that I don't need a greenhouse to survive. I can grow anywhere.

The Bee's Visit

No flower can survive entirely on its own. Even the strongest "Single Stem" needs a visit from a bee now and then. In nature, bees bring the pollen that allows for new life. In my life, the "Bees" are the people who help me heal—my therapist, my family, my true friends.

Accepting help was one of the hardest things for me. My "Thorns" wanted to keep everyone away, and my "Armor of Petals" wanted to convince everyone I didn't need anything. But I've realized that therapy isn't a sign of weakness; it's a form of "Cross-Pollination." It's bringing in new ideas, new perspectives, and new tools to help my roots get stronger.

I am learning to welcome the visit. I am opening up my "Internal Root" to the people who actually want to help me garden. I am realizing that by letting someone else in, I am not losing my independence; I am gaining the strength I need to bloom. We are all part of an ecosystem. I help the bees, and the bees help me.

Stretching Upward

Every morning, a plant has to make a choice. It has to stretch upward, moving against the force of gravity to find the sun. When you live with depression, "Stretching Upward" is a literal struggle. It's the physical effort it takes to push back the covers, get out of bed, and face the day.

Some days, the stretch is easy. Other days, it feels like I'm trying to move through concrete. But the act of reaching is what makes the stem strong. Every time I choose to try, I am building "emotional muscle." I am teaching my body that I am in charge, not the "Weighted Root."

I'm learning not to judge how far I stretch. Some days, stretching upward just means taking a shower. Other days, it means going to school and finishing all my work. Both are victories. As long as I am still reaching, I am still alive. I am a work in progress, and the effort of the reach is more important than the height I achieve.

Open Petals

In the "Visible Bloom" section, we talked about the mask. But in the "Healing" section, we talk about "Open Petals." This is the vulnerability of finally being honest about who you are. It's the moment you stop saying "I'm fine" and start saying "I'm struggling, but I'm working on it."

Opening up is terrifying. When your petals are open, your heart is exposed. You are vulnerable to the "Sudden Frost" and the "Pollinated Gossip." But you are also finally able to feel the real sun. You can't receive love or support if you are permanently closed up in a "Paper Flower" shell.

I am practicing being open. I am telling my truth to the people who have earned the right to hear it. I am finding that when I open my petals, other people do, too. We realize that we are all just stems trying to survive. Authenticity is the only thing that actually heals the "Internal Root." I am done hiding. I am ready to be seen.

Rooted and Grounded

Anxiety makes you feel like you are floating—disconnected from your body and the world around you. Healing is the process of getting "Rooted and Grounded." It's the practice of mindfulness, of coming back to the present moment and feeling the earth beneath your feet.

I use "Grounding Techniques" like roots. When my mind starts to race into the "Midnight Petals" of the future, I force myself to name five things I can see. I feel the texture of my clothes. I listen to the sound of my own breath. I am anchoring myself to the *now*. I am reminding my brain that the past is over and the future hasn't happened yet.

Being grounded doesn't mean you don't feel the wind; it just means the wind can't blow you away. I am finding a sense of stability that I never thought I could have. I am a single stem, but I am firmly planted. I am here. I am safe. I am home.

The Garden Gate

A healthy garden needs a gate. You have to decide who gets to walk through your rows and who has to stay on the other side of the fence. This is the essay about boundaries. For a long time, I let people trample over my "Hidden Roots" because I didn't want to be "difficult." I let them pick my petals and break my branches because I wanted to be liked.

But a flower with no boundaries eventually dies. I am learning to set the "Garden Gate." I am saying "no" to things that drain me. I am telling people how I need to be treated. I am realizing that my peace is more important than their approval.

The gate isn't about being mean; it's about being healthy. When I have good boundaries, I have more to give to the people who actually care about me. I am protecting my "Single Stem" so that I can keep growing for a long time. My garden is a sacred space, and I am the only one who holds the key.

Sunlight on the Stem

We spend so much time focusing on the bloom that we forget the stem—the part of us that holds everything together. "Sunlight on the Stem" is about self-love. It's about appreciating your own strength, your own resilience, and your own journey.

I am learning to look in the mirror and see more than just my "Thorns" or my "Wilt." I am seeing a person who has survived things that would have broken someone else. I am seeing a person who is brave enough to be vulnerable. I am feeling the warmth of my own self-acceptance.

I am worthy of the sun. I am worthy of the water. I am worthy of the space I take up in this world. This isn't "Perfume of Positivity"—it's a deep, internal knowing. I am a single stem, and I am enough exactly as I am. I don't need to be a different kind of flower to be valuable. I am Ja'Shaun, and I am blooming.

Cross-Pollination

As I reach the end of this book, I am thinking about "Cross-Pollination." This is the moment where my story leaves my garden and enters yours. By sharing my struggles with PTSD, anxiety, and depression, I am hoping to carry a little bit of hope to someone else who is still stuck in the "Dark Basement."

Sharing your story is a form of healing. It turns your "Thorns" into tools for connection. When I hear someone else say, "I feel that too," the "Soil of Silence" gets a little bit thinner. We are all connected by our struggles and our growth.

I am no longer ashamed of my "Two Sides." I realize that by being honest about my "Hidden Roots," I am giving someone else permission to be honest about theirs. We are creating a bigger garden together—one where everyone is allowed to be messy, and everyone is allowed to heal. My story is just one stem, but together, we are a field of wildflowers.

The Single Stem

This is the final essay, and it brings us back to the title: *Two Sides of a Single Stem*. Throughout this journey, we've looked at the "Hidden Roots" and the "Visible Bloom." We've felt the "Thorns" and we've reached for the "Sun." For a long time, I thought these were two different people. I thought I had to choose which one to be.

But now I know the truth. You can't have the bloom without the roots. You can't have the strength without the struggle. I am both the person who cries in the dark and the person who laughs in the light. I am both the survivor and the striver. I am a single, unified being. Healing isn't about getting rid of one side; it's about accepting the whole stem. It's about realizing that the "Two Sides" are what make me beautiful. I am standing tall today, not because I am perfect, but because I am integrated. I am rooted in my history and reaching for my future. I am Ja'Shaun Coley, and this is my garden. And even if the seasons change, I know that I have everything I need, right here on this single stem

About the Author

Jashaun is a 17-year-old author from North Carolina who writes with raw honesty about his journey through mental health. His work reflects the struggles, strength, and self-discovery of a young mind navigating complex emotions. Through storytelling, Jashaun hopes to connect with others who feel unseen and remind them that their voice - and their story - matters.

www.ingramcontent.com/pod-product-compliance
Lightning Source LLC
LaVergne TN
LVHW022321200926
848481LV00004B/1394

* 9 7 9 8 2 3 3 1 5 8 8 3 4 *